I0390719

For contact purposes.

You could reach us through the email address:

highway2wisdom@gmail.com

Contact us. Tell us your testimony.

You could also send in your prayer requests, questions and your thoughts also. We are very much delighted to pray with you, answer your questions and reply your comments and messages.

ACKNOWLEDGEMENTS

To me, acknowledgement is a really tasking part of writing a book, in that it is very easy to unknowingly leave out, or omit a very important name. By God's grace, I will do as much as I can to recognize and acknowledge everyone that was a part of the success of this book.

Firstly, all thanks and gratitude to God for seeing this book to the end, never failing to pour our the requested and required inspiration for it. I also acknowledge my pastor Dr. Paul Enenche, senior pastor, Dunamis International Gospel Center Worldwide, for his teachings, as it was a pillar of support for this book.

Time will fail me to talk about the immense support and encouragement I had from my friend Kendra Blessing. I would not forget my brother Moses Zion for his commitment and encouraging words.

I celebrate the likes of a mentor and dear man of God, Prophet O. Solomon, for his divine insight and release of prophetic words leading to the adept writing of this book.

TABLE OF CONTENTS

FORWARD

The concept of being wealthy is one subject on the mind of all adults, even teens; almost everyone. Everybody wants to become rich, wealthy, influential and all that, but not everybody is rich, wealthy and influential. Why? For two reasons: One is, not everyone fully knows how. The other is, some has the knowledge, they know how, but has not put it to adequate test, or are too lazy to apply it in their daily lives.

This book opens our eyes to ageless truth as to how wealth is created. The principles therein are so clear, unambiguous and very precise they it strikes a cord in you spirit as you keep on reading. This book makes us understand how easy it is to create wealth, and not just that, it gives us a clear understanding as to how we can create a "lasting" wealth.

It is one thing to be wealthy, and it is another thing to stay wealthy. As you meditatively study this well inspired book, you will come to understand how being wealthy is your right and how staying wealthy is unbelievably easy.

- A. B. Chuks

INTRODUCTION

The subject of money is one of the most common issues in the world today. It is a daily necessity in the lives of everyone. It make life either easier or very unbearable, depending on it's availability.

In the times we live, money has become a god. People are change by it, so drastically that the former becomes so different and unrecognizable from the latter. No wonder the Bible says the love of it is the root of all evil.

1 Timothy 6:10

For the love of money is the root of all evil: which while some coveted after, they have erred from the faith, and pierced themselves through with many sorrows.

- Kjv

A lot of people have misinterpreted this passage of the scripture. They now abhor and criticize money and the people in possession of it. It is very paramount to note that there is a clear difference between a master and a servant. There is a distinct difference between a man that has control over money and a man that is under the control of money, thereby becoming a slave to it.

We were created in the image of God. The heaven is filled with precious stones and beauty unimaginable. Why do we then settle for less as children of the most high God here on earth? No! This is not meant to be so.

The Bible declares:

> 2 Corinthians 8:9
>
> For ye know the grace of our Lord Jesus Christ, that, though he was rich, yet for your sakes he became poor, that ye through his poverty might be rich.

- Kjv

Jesus died on the cross, to solve all our problems. This is not excluding our financial problems. Though he was rich, but he became poor so that you and I can become rich in all things. So, don't you think it is an insult and a waste of Christ's death for you on the cross if you are still poor? Come to think of it, Jesus did not only die on the cross to make you righteous, so you can be able to go to heaven. No! He also died to heal you, to deliver you, to also bless your finances and end that money struggle in your life.

As we deal on the subject of money, we

will also understand the subject of wealth creation. How we can magnet money and allow it work for us as we want, while still remaining in control, making it our slave and we masters.

Money is so important even in the work of God that Solomon, the most wise King said:

> *Ecclesiastes 10:19*
>
> *A feast is made for laughter, and wine maketh merry: but money answereth all things.*
>
> *- Kjv*

Ecclesiastes 7:12

For wisdom is a defence, and money is a defence...

- Kjv

So if you are there thinking, or have had the notion that money is a taboo or too much money is a sin, maybe... just maybe, that is the reason why you don't have it.

You can never attract what you attack. You can never contact what you counter. What you don't celebrate will never elevate you.

- Dr. Paul Enenche

The Bible made us understand vividly what the problem is. It didn't say that money is the root of all evil, instead it says that "the love" of money is the root of all evil. Buttressing this, we can say that the love of money is what makes a man cheat his neighbor, steal, kill and do other evil act, just to have it. But money in itself is not, and will never be evil.

As we delve more into this well inspired book, filled with ageless truths, we would come to understand how being blessed financially is our right as sons and daughters of the most high God and how much He wants us to live a poverty free life.

CHAPTER ONE

What is poverty?

Let us start by stating the dictionary definition of poverty.

According to the English Oxford dictionary, poverty is:

1. *Any deficiency of elements or resources that are needed or desired, or that constitute richness; as, poverty of the soil; poverty of the blood; poverty of ideas.*

2. *It is also the quality or state of being*

in want, or in scarcity.

Notice what the dictionary meaning implies, that it is the state of being "deficient of resources". As true as this can be, I want to bring our notice to the further meaning of poverty.

Poverty as we would be studying, is not just the state of being deficient of resources, but it is a state of being deficient, in the mind. If it is lacking in the physical, but not in your mind, give it time, what is in your mind will surely be made manifest, it will sure materialize in the physical, corroborating what you always had in your mind, or what you have always seen in your mind's eyes.

Note that if it is lacking in your mind, even though it is present in the physical at the moment, give it time, it will soon vanish. It will soon agree with what you have in your thought. For the physical is controlled by the metaphysical. What is made manifest is controlled by the supernatural, by the weight of our thoughts.

A man can have nothing in his bank account at the moment, but if he still has vision, and hope is still alive to do better, to have more, then, that man is not poor. He is just not having what he is meant to at the moment, but his hope and drive will surely make surplus available in no time, if he persist. Take note of that word "if". It is a condition that must be met. If he stops on the way, he will not see that desired result. So the key is to persist and not give up on the way.

Poverty is a state of the mind. You are only poor when you have given up all hope to succeed, when you are completely worn-out, beaten, bent over and have lost the will to continue.

It does not matter how many times a man fails, he is still not a failure. What makes a man a failure is when he fails and gives up on rising again; when he falls down and decides to stay down flat. That is only when a man can be called a failure.

Poverty is the will of a man that has been broken and crushed; that has been conditioned never to rise again.

The circumstances of life around him has chocked the will and drive to continue. But let me tell that man something, "it is not what happens around you that should drive you or determine what should become of you, but what bubbles on the inside of you; the drive to do better, to reach higher, to accomplish greater, THAT, should be your driving force".

So if you still have the will and strength on the inside of you to fight on, to accomplish greater, don't worry, you are not poor, time will bring to you all you desire. Keep on doing all that is necessary, keep on doing the things you will come to learn from our subsequent study, the principles laid down in this book, and I tell you, not for so long, you will swim in abundance, so much so that you become a wonder, even to yourself.

CHAPTER TWO

What is wealth?

Let us also see the dictionary definition and meaning of wealth.

Wealth according to the English Oxford dictionary is:

1. *Riches; valuable material possessions.*

2. *A great amount; an abundance or plenty.*

3. *Welfare; prosperity; good; well-being.*

This dictionary meaning talks about visible material. It brings our consciousness to the things that we need and want that are made available as at when we desire them to be.

As true as that would be, let me also bring our consciousness to a yet deeper meaning of wealth.

Wealth is not calculated by the acquisition of a man; how much money he has in his bank account, the number of cars in his garage, the number of women at his beck and call -and vice-versa, or what his company or empire is worth.

That man or woman can have all these things and still be poor. You see, wealth is not in the acquisition but in the acknowledgement and contentment.

So a man can have little, but if that man acknowledges what he has, thereby having contentment, then, that man is wealthy.

Being wealthy, is having all there is to have, and including the most important "desert" to it -Peace. Peace of mind is what make all the possessions of a man mean something to him. When there's no peace, there is no contentment, and where there is no contentment, then the idea of being truly wealthy has already been defeated.

Furthermore, true wealth is not in the quantity of acquisition, but in the quality of influence of those acquisition. A man is not said to be rich if what he possesses has not affected the lives and destinies of the less privileged. By saying the less privileged, I mean those that are deficient of what he possess and would need it to progress or advance in life, career, finance, relationships, ministry and so on.

You might have "little", but if that "little" can affect the life of even one person, you are truly rich. Trust me, in no time, you will truly have all you require and more, so you can meet more need, and spread your help and giving tentacles. God sure makes good of his promises.

> *Luke 6:38*
>
> *Give, and it shall be given unto you; good measure, pressed down, and shaken together, and running over, shall men give into your bosom. For with the same measure that ye mete withal it shall be measured to you again.*
>
> *- Kjv*

So a man's real worth is not in the quantity and quality of his possessions, but in the people and lives his "wealth" has affected positively, in one way or another.

Furthermore, a good name, they saying, is more valuable than silver and gold. A good name can bring a man where money cannot.

Proverbs 22:1

A good name is rather to be chosen than great riches, and loving favour rather than silver and gold.

- Kjv

Ecclesiastes 7:1

A good name is better than precious ointment...

- *Kjv*

Therefore, we can say that a man that has a good name is said to be even more valuable than a man that has everything, even if he feeds the poor and affect the lives of the less privileged with his wealth.

This will bring us to the next chapter of this book, where we will be studying and learning how we can move from being "physically" poor to being "physically" wealthy. Also we would understand how to move from being "mentally" poor, to bring "mentally" rich, giving rise to the metaphysical being made manifest.

CHAPTER THREE

How to activate wealth

There are diverse ways that wealth can be activated in one's life, or can be amplified as the case may be.

We are going to study all of the laid down principles of wealth creation.

Wealth is very easy to acquire, if and only if these principles can be followed, not partially or inconsistently, but religiously and tenaciously. Remember:

In consistency lies the power.
- Gloria Copland.

Hosea 6:3

Then shall we know, if we follow on to know...

- Kjv

It is very important to note, as we continue, that it is not in the "knowing" alone, but in the "application" of that which is "known". For what a man knows is not as important as what he does with that knowledge.

You see, there is a very big emphasis on "application" of knowledge, which is also called "doing" in the scripture. For there is no difference between a man that reads and knows all things, but does not apply that knowledge of his, with a man that lacks the ability to read and therefore knows not.

This is why it is written:

Matthew 5:19

...but whosoever shall do and teach them, the same shall be called great in the kingdom of heaven.

- Kjv

James 1:22

But be ye doers of the word, and not hearers only, deceiving your own selves.

- Kjv

Acts 1:1

The former treatise have I made, O Theophilus, of all that Jesus began both to do and teach,

- Kjv

So as we study these principles of wealth creation, it is therefore not in the knowledge of them only, but in the application that makes the difference.

Principles Of Wealth Creation

There are various principles of wealth creation, we are going to study them one after another.

1.Acknowledge that you have something.

A lot of times, most people fail to understand that there is no one born into this world that has nothing.

The creator made sure of this. It is left for all to first understand that there is something that they have and therefore they can multiply.

This is the first principle of wealth creation. For if a man fails to acknowledge that he has something, he will definitely be oblivious of the fact that that substance he has got, can be multiplied, and the thought of wealth creation from the inside of him, projecting to the outside, becoming visible and a reality, will seem abstract and alien to his shallow thought.

Let us sight an explanation of this truth in the scripture.

Matthew 25:15

And unto one he gave five talents, to another two, and to another one; to every man according to his several ability...

- Kjv

It is also worthy of note that everyone is giving something that he can enhance, build upon and multiply, ACCORDING TO HIS ABILITY.

Everyone's ability is on a different level. You have to find out what you have, and multiply it, then more even would be given to you.

Do not try to envy anyone's abilities, gifting, skill or potentials. YOU HAVE GOT YOURS! Use it. For when you do, then you are diligent and grateful, and the Father multiplies it.

Let us see further, the above scripture, it will explain the benefits of being grateful for what you have, and multiplying it, and also the dangers of being ungrateful and "hiding" your "talent"(potentials).

Matthew 25:16-29

Then he that had received the five talents went and traded with the same, and made them other five talents.

17. And likewise he that had received two, he also gained other two.

18. But he that had received one went and digged in the earth, and hid his lord's money.

19. After a long time the lord of those servants cometh, and reckoneth with them.

20. And so he that had received five talents came and brought other five talents, saying, Lord, thou deliveredst unto me five talents: behold, I have gained beside them five talents more.

21. His lord said unto him, Well

done, thou good and faithful servant: thou hast been faithful over a few things, I will make thee ruler over many things: enter thou into the joy of thy lord.

22. He also that had received two talents came and said, Lord, thou deliveredst unto me two talents: behold, I have gained two other talents beside them.

23. His lord said unto him, Well done, good and faithful servant; thou hast been faithful over a few things, I will make thee ruler over many things: enter thou into the joy of thy lord.

24. Then he which had received the one talent came and said,

Lord, I knew thee that thou art an hard man, reaping where thou hast not sown, and gathering where thou hast not strawed:

25. And I was afraid, and went and hid thy talent in the earth: lo, there thou hast that is thine.

26. His lord answered and said unto him, Thou wicked and slothful servant, thou knewest that I reap where I sowed not, and gather where I have not strawed:

27. Thou oughtest therefore to have put my money to the exchangers, and then at my coming I should have received mine own with usury.

28. Take therefore the talent from

him, and give it unto him which hath ten talents.

29. For unto every one that hath shall be given, and he shall have abundance: but from him that hath not shall be taken away even that which he hath.

- kjv

We can clearly see the benefits and dangers of multiplying our God-given potentials and ignoring them, respectively.

As we see in the passage we read above, he that has, will be given more, and he that has not, from him will be taken even that which he has. Meaning that everyone has something, whether they choose to believe it, and therefore see it, or not. Also, if you multiple what you have, you will grow momentum and capacity to have even more, but if you believe and feel you have not, the little sparkles of potentials inside out you, will fade away ,having no one to rekindle it. So that which you have will then be taken away and given to the man that has.

When this man that seeks to multiply what he has does so, he begins to grow capacity and more ideas begins to come to him, he will in no distant time, venture into that business line meant for the man that feels he has not. He will in no distant time come up with that idea to make a metallic container, holding actual humans fly in the air called aeroplane, he'll soon discover that man can go to the moon, and soon will expand as he grows capacity that man can maybe live and survive in another planet other than the earth.

This is definitely how man has been structured. A lazy man will never know what he would have accomplished if he gets to work. And a hardworking man would always scale new heights, not probably because he was designed for that leap, but he utilized what he has, so he grows capacity for more, he grows capacity to take over what belongs to the "lazy" man; the man that feels he has not.

Remember:

> *Luke 16:10*
>
> *He that is faithful in that which is least is faithful also in much: and he that is unjust in the least is unjust also in much.*
>
> *- Kjv*

This explains to us that a man that is seen to be faithful in the "little" thing committed into his care, will also do well, if much is entrusted to him. Also in the same vein, he that is not faithful in the "little" things committed into his hands, will do same if much is entrusted to him.

A lot of people feel that what they have, the position they occupy in the office, the amount of shares they control, the estate they manage, the property they assess, the money they have, is too small. They feel they "deserve" something more or better. Well, maybe they do, but if that which is committed into your hand is in a "sorry" state, if that which is entrusted to you is lacking your best touch, then you have made yourself unqualified for the bigger responsibility, you have made yourself unfit for that promotion.

Manage what you have well, and it will be glaring to all that you are fit and due for a lifting.

Remember:

Ecclesiastes 9:10

Whatsoever thy hand findeth to do, do it with thy might...

- Kjv

Proverbs 22:29

Seest thou a man diligent in his

business? he shall stand before kings; he shall not stand before mean men.

- Kjv

So this is rule number one. Acknowledge that you have got something to offer to your generation. Agree that there is something that you have got to give, and subsequently multiple, then and only then can you qualify for the wealth creating ability.

2. Give thanks when it seems not enough.

The ability to be grateful at all times is truly a virtue. Have you ever felt like what you have is not enough to cater for your needs?

Have you ever wanted to throw in the towel? Have you ever felt like giving up? Not for any flimsy excuse, but because you do not have enough money for your tuition fees, to feed yourself or your family through the "winter", to give proper care to your family, to complete that mortgage payment, to give your family that long overdue vacation, to complete your rent payment, not enough resources to complete that project?

Have you ever felt like committing suicide, taking your own life because you feel you can't meet up?

Yes. Sometimes you might feel that way, not because you have no right to, but because you are actually in a pretty beat -up and messed-up situation and you have every right to feel like giving up. But you know what? DO NOT GIVE UP! There is always a way out.

Let us see some scriptural examples where resources were lacking, and what transpired afterwards to cause an overflow.

Matthew 14:15-20

15. And when it was evening, his

disciples came to him, saying, This is a desert place, and the time is now past; send the multitude away, that they may go into the villages, and buy themselves victuals.

16. But Jesus said unto them, They need not depart; give ye them to eat.

17. And they say unto him, We have here but five loaves, and two fishes.

18. He said, Bring them hither to me.

19. And he commanded the multitude to sit down on the grass, and took the five loaves, and the two fishes, and looking up to

heaven, he blessed, and brake, and gave the loaves to his disciples, and the disciples to the multitude.

20. And they did all eat, and were filled: and they took up of the fragments that remained twelve baskets full.

- kjv

In this scriptural reverence, we can see so many things worthy of note.

Let us talk about one of them.

Jesus saw that the multitude needed to eat, he did not say, "let us go look for a bakery that can accommodate and cater for five thousand men, excluding women and children". He knew they had something. He knew they had something to build on. He didn't care how "small" people think it was, to him, it was more that enough.

I could sense the discipline thinking "oh man! What does Jesus think he is doing? Does he know for sure how many we are here? Does he know that we have only got five loaves and two fishes? Think about this Jesus before you make a mess of yourself and your ministry! This is insane! It is in no way 'rational'! It is illogical! It in no way satisfy the law of nature!"

Yes! This is why we do not operate in

the law of the physical realm, we operate a higher law! Glory to God! We operate the law that govern the heavens. We are supernatural!

If only we could be thankful and be appreciative for the "little" we've got, it will surely multiply.

Jesus knew this. He knew all he had to do was to thank God for what was present at the moment, and He will multiply it to meet the present need.

Jesus gave thanks, and as "small" as five loaves and two fishes were, it fed five thousand people -excluding women and children. It was more that enough, so much so that everyone ate to their satisfaction and twelve baskets were gathered up as remnant. Wow! What a mighty God we serve.

If you can only be grateful for the "little" you have, if you could only be thankful for what seems not enough, it will surely multiply. Why? Because if you are thankful for the little, you qualify for the much.

3. Follow the leading, direction and instructions from God.

It is of utmost importance that we follow that direction, instructions and leading from the Holy Spirit.

What is made manifest, what we can see, is mostly controlled, orchestrated and birthed from the supernatural. So if we want to survive in the physical, it is expedient for us to know what is current in the realm of the supernatural (spirit, metaphysical).

Most of the time, what we see as OK, the business idea we think is amazing and nothing will stop from going global, might just turn of to be what will wear us out. This is why we have to know what will thrive in the physical, by putting on the lens of the supernatural and checking it from that perspective.

Always, when we listen hard enough, we will hear what God is telling us to do, the step He is asking us to take, the decision that seem insane He is asking us to make. It might defy every natural logic and reasoning, but that is why the realm of the supernatural is so different from the realm of the physical.

Let us see some practical examples from the scriptures.

John 2:1-10

1. And the third day there was a marriage in Cana of Galilee; and the mother of Jesus was there:

2. And both Jesus was called, and his disciples, to the marriage.

3. And when they wanted wine, the mother of Jesus saith unto him, They have no wine.

4. Jesus saith unto her, Woman, what have I to do with thee? mine hour is not yet come.

5. His mother saith unto the servants, Whatsoever he saith unto you, do it.

6. And there were set there six waterpots of stone, after the manner of the purifying of the Jews, containing two or three firkins apiece.

7. Jesus saith unto them, Fill the

waterpots with water. And they filled them up to the brim.

8. And he saith unto them, Draw out now, and bear unto the governor of the feast. And they bare it.

9. When the ruler of the feast had tasted the water that was made wine, and knew not whence it was: (but the servants which drew the water knew;) the governor of the feast called the bridegroom,

10. And saith unto him, Every man at the beginning doth set forth good wine; and when men have well drunk, then that which is worse: but thou hast kept the good wine until now.

In this scriptural reference, we see how what was thought to be impossible was made possible by obedience to instruction. The wine was not enough, the guests needed more. Mary, the mother of Jesus, enquired of her son, for she knew who He was and what he can do. She therefore told the servants that whatever Jesus ask them to do, they should do without hesitation. She didn't bother to know or enquire what Jesus would tell them, she just knew that as long as the instruction is coming for him, no matter how "insane" and unrealistic it might seem, it is surly what would help their situation.

So they obeyed. Imagine how illogical that instruction is. Jesus ask them to fill the six jars with water. Water?! Seriously?! They need wine not water!!! But with God all things are possible, if we can believe and follow the instruction we receive, no matter how "stupid" it seems to us.

According to the scripture we just saw, those jars of water became the best wine the guest drank that day, and possibly the best they ever drank. Glory to God!

Also let us consider this scriptural

reference.

Matthew 14:15-20

15. And when it was evening, his disciples came to him, saying, This is a desert place, and the time is now past; send the multitude away, that they may go into the villages, and buy themselves victuals.

16. But Jesus said unto them, They need not depart; give ye them to eat.

17. And they say unto him, We have here but five loaves, and two fishes.

18. He said, Bring them hither to

me.

19. And he commanded the multitude to sit down on the grass, and took the five loaves, and the two fishes, and looking up to heaven, he blessed, and brake, and gave the loaves to his disciples, and the disciples to the multitude.

20. And they did all eat, and were filled: and they took up of the fragments that remained twelve baskets full.

- Kjv

As we read this passage above, we would notice the strategic instruction

Jesus gave to the multitude before they got feed. He asked them to settle down on the grass. He asked them to sit. It was an instruction, a strategic one at that. If some amongst them had said "we have no food here, and he is asking us to sit. For what?! Please am out of here". If anyone had thought so, and acted on that thought, they would have been left out of the supernatural provision that came next.

Most times in our lives, all we need for that next lifting, for that quantum leap, is to obey the instruction, direction, and leading of the Holy Spirit.

God is always saying something. For us

to receive his touch in any area of our lives, there must be a willingness and ability to obey his leading and instruction.

I know at this juncture, it is being noted that for one to follow the instructions and Leadings of God, one must first of all be able to hear him, know it is Him speaking, and also be able to interpret His voice.

So now, some of you might say "how do I know when God is speaking?" Or "how can I hear the voice of God and know it?". Well, it's quite easy. Actually, easier than breathing.

I can not comprehensively deal on that study now, it is a separate subject on it's own. Not to worry, if you have no clue as to how to hear God's voice, interpret it and put it into profitable use, there is already a book titled "HOW TO HEAR GOD" by O. C. Everest. You can read that, I assure you that your questions would be answered.

4. Have total confidence that God will always provide for you.

What is confidence? I want us to start from the definition of that word "confidence".

Well, according to the English language dictionary, confidence can be said to be the expression or feeling of CERTAINTY, the quality of TRUSTING. It is also said to be SELF-ASSURANCE about someone or something.

Now when we talk about "total" confidence that God will always provide for us, we are simply talking about having unconditional trust in the all sufficiently of God, to cater and provide for our need. We are indeed referring to the unwavering self-assurance that God is big enough to prove himself in our finances.

Let me give a befitting illustration of this

subject matter.

God, in the scripture said:

> *1 Timothy 5:8*
>
> *But if any provide not for his own, and specially for those of his own house, he hath denied the faith, and is worse than an infidel.*
>
> *- Kjv*

Now, if God could tell us this, if He admonishes all believers to take care of their family, do you think that He would not live and lead by example? Do you think that He will not take care of his own? Oh yes! He will surely take care of you.

Remember what He said again:

Matthew 6:25-32

25. Therefore I say unto you, Take no thought for your life, what ye shall eat, or what ye shall drink; nor yet for your body, what ye shall put on. Is not the life more than meat, and the body than raiment?

26. Behold the fowls of the air: for they sow not, neither do they reap, nor gather into barns; yet your heavenly Father feedeth them. Are ye not much better than they?

27. Which of you by taking thought can add one cubit unto

his stature?

28. And why take ye thought for raiment? Consider the lilies of the field, how they grow; they toil not, neither do they spin:

29. And yet I say unto you, That even Solomon in all his glory was not arrayed like one of these.

30. Wherefore, if God so clothe the grass of the field, which to day is, and to morrow is cast into the oven, shall he not much more clothe you, O ye of little faith?

31. Therefore take no thought, saying, What shall we eat? or, What shall we drink? or, Wherewithal shall we be clothed?

32. (For after all these things do the Gentiles seek:) for your heavenly Father knoweth that ye have need of all these things.

- Kjv

Do you know that it is an insult to the sufficiently of God for you to worry?

This is what it means when you worry. When you worry, you are telling God that He is not capable enough to take care of you. You are literally saying that God needs your help to plan your survival, that He is not doing His job properly and therefore, you have come to supervise Him and help Him do His job.

How insulting this can be. It is very important to note and always remember that God will always provide for His children. He is a loving Father, He can never abandon His sons and daughters.

Sometimes, it feels like God has abandoned us, it feels as though He is not keeping to his words. Sometimes we could feel like He is so far He can not hear our cry.

Well, let me break it down to you. God will never fail!

The psalmist David said:

Paul the apostle also said:

God then said in His word:

Psalms 89:34-35

My covenant will I not break, nor alter the thing that is gone out of my lips.

Once have I sworn by my holiness that I will not lie...

God can never lie about what He has promised. If He has said it, surely He will do it. The issue is never with God. The issue is always with us. That is why He said, and it is written in the scripture:

Hosea 4:6

My people are destroyed for lack

of knowledge...

- Kjv

As we see clearly in the above scripture, God was referring to His children; believers, not unbelievers. He said His children perish, not because of any other thing, but because they "lack" knowledge.

So you can be born again, tongue talking and spirit filled, but if you lack the knowledge God talks about, and the application, then you might also fail like "ordinary" men. Success is all about having the required knowledge and applying it where necessary.

Wealth creation is achieved by following the laid down principles. There is no "abracadabra" about it. It is simple, if you follow the laid down principles, DEDICATEDLY and CONSISTENTLY, you will surely arrive at the predicted result.

5. Do something; Faith without works is dead.

In this subtopic, we would be dealing with a rather delicate issue. This is the area most believers fail. To magnet wealth and success, you have to DO something. There has to be an action backed up with your unwavering faith in

God that you will succeed at it.

The point most believers still do not get is that, one can be Spirit filled, tongue talking, demon casting and so on, and still be poor, looking battered, shattered and scattered. It is all about following the principles. No amount of fasting and prayer can make a lazy or an idle man succeed.

The truth is, "manna" has finished falling since the time of Moses and the Israelites in the wilderness. It will not fall again. Am I saying that there are no times God gives us a miracle of unexplainable money appearing in People's bank account or mysteriously in their possession? No!

All I am trying to establish here is that a believer in Christ Jesus ought not to totally live and depend on "miracle money". God can choose to show up for us in that manner if He chooses to, but that would be to meet a particular need of ours at that time, and not to depend on that everyday for the rest of our lives, that would be the height of laziness. If one has this mindset, one would greatly be disappointed.

Fasting and praying alone cannot, and will not guarantee you wealth and success, but prayer and fasting, backed up with FAITH and ACTION, following the laid down principles will.

The scripture says in psalms 1:

> *Psalms 1:3*
>
> *And he shall be like a tree planted by the rivers of water, that bringeth forth his fruit in his season; his leaf also shall not wither; and whatsoever he doeth shall prosper.*
>
> *- Kjv*

> *Deuteronomy 2:7*
>
> *For the LORD thy God hath blessed thee in all the works of*

thy hand...

- Kjv

Looking at those highlighted phrases closely, we see that God is trying to tell us that for your prosperity to be evident, you have got to do something. He has to see something to bless when He comes for you. An empty hands cannot be multiplied. According to mathematics, zero times zero is equal to zero ($0*0= 0$). Something has to be available to be multiplied and to increase and be prosperous.

The scripture also declares:

Proverbs 6:9-11

9. How long wilt thou sleep, O sluggard? when wilt thou arise out of thy sleep?

10. Yet a little sleep, a little slumber, a little folding of the hands to sleep:

11. So shall thy poverty come as one that travelleth, and thy want as an armed man.

- kjv

Proverbs 13:4

The soul of the sluggard desireth, and hath nothing: but the soul of the diligent shall be made fat.

Proverbs 20:4

The sluggard will not plow by reason of the cold; therefore shall he beg in harvest, and have nothing.

- Kjv

All what these scriptures are telling us is the need to be active, the need to "do something" and not be idle or lazy.

The Bible says in the book of James:

James 2:20

But wilt thou know, O vain man, that faith without works is dead?

- Kjv

James 2:26

For as the body without the spirit is dead, so faith without works is dead also.

- Kjv

This utterly means that you cannot sit idle, lazing around but fasting and praying fervently that your bank account will be filled with money. That would be totally against the rules and principles of wealth creation acknowledged by God himself.

When you fast and pray for growth and increase in your finances, there must be a backing, a willingness and an ongoing commitment, doing something substantial. Then, and only then can the works of your hands be blessed.

6. Let what you do glorify God.

God is interested in our business. God is so interested in all that we do. Of course He is, He is our Father after all, and wish his children to prosper.

The secret here is letting all you do, letting your ideas and business plans please and glorify God.

For instance, God will never be involved in the financial uplifting of prostitution as a form of career. He will never endorse quantum leap in finances in the area of fraud as a "business".

Most people do no take this into consideration. They do the things they are not meant to do and pray for God to increase them. That is so contradictory to the qualities, character and personality of God.

I was in a church meeting one day, and I heard the pastor preaching on the subject of evil money. He told his experience. He came from a country that is well known worldwide for fraudulent activities. So there he was sitting in an airport in another country, a young man was sitting with him. The young man, noticing that he was a well renowned pastor, recognized him because they were fellow countrymen. Told him to please pray for his "hustle" as he called it. So while the pastor was about to pray that God prospers him, asked him what he does. To the shock of all, he said "I traffic hard drugs".

What?! "Hard drugs"?! Can you imagine? How can someone expect God to bless such a business idea. That substance aids murder, chaos and so many social vices you can think of. How can our beloved Father aid such a line of work?

It is then very expedient to note that you cannot expect God to act on your finances if what you do does not please him or give him glory. If what you do pleases Him, He will surely make it prosper. For even the scripture says:

> *Proverbs 16:7*
>
> *When a man's ways please the LORD, he maketh even his enemies to be at peace with him.*
>
> *- Kjv*

This is literally showing us how God moves on things that concerns us, when those things pleases him and gives Him pleasure.

7. Giving

The scripture declares:

> *Ecclesiastes 11:1*
>
> *Cast thy bread upon the waters: for thou shalt find it after many days.*
>
> *- Kjv*

> *Luke 6:38*
>
> *Give, and it shall be given unto you; good measure, pressed down, and shaken together, and running over, shall men give into your bosom. For with the same measure that*

ye mete withal it shall be measured to you again.

- Kjv

2 Corinthians 9:7

Every man according as he purposeth in his heart, so let him give; not grudgingly, or of necessity: for God loveth a cheerful giver.

- Kjv

In Christianity as a way of life, giving is a core practice that must be upheld. It all started from our Father, He is our number one role model. We learn from Him.

The Bible declares in the book of John:

> *John 3:16*
>
> *For God so loved the world, that he gave his only begotten Son, that whosoever believeth in him should not perish, but have everlasting life.*
>
> *- Kjv*

This practice was first demonstrated by God our Father, to show how important it is. It goes to prove how much you love, and this in turn moves the hand of God to intervene in your finances.

It is very important to note as we continue that we do not give because we want an increase in our finances or that we want something in return, that would be gross manipulation. We give because we have been given and because we love. This in turn culminates into abundant flow of supply in return.

I have never seen a broke giver. I have never seen a poor generous man. This is the principle that so many people practice, some, unknowing to them, and they are so wealthy, and you wonder how. This law is a universal law. If you give, surely it shall be given unto you.

But as believers, we give not because

we are forced to, or because we want something in return, we give because that is our nature, the nature of God the Father. The generous One.

Matthew 5:45

That ye may be the children of your Father which is in heaven: for he maketh his sun to rise on the evil and on the good, and sendeth rain on the just and on the unjust.

- Kjv

This act of unconditional generosity of believers moves the resultant effect of the principle of giving to be evident in the believer's life.

It is a matter of following judiciously the principle of giving and seeing the result manifest.

8. Confess the right confession.

As believers in Christ Jesus, our confession is very powerful. What we say with our mouth determines our outcome in life and destiny. You cannot keep saying that you will die and expect to live. Let me go a little deeper into this ageless truth, but before we give scriptural references, let me tell you a little bit, real life experiences about this subject of how powerful our confession is.

An experiment was conducted by several renowned people you could google about, to determine if truly our words are powerful or not. A bowl of rice was cooked, and served into different transparent containers. On one of this container was written "love", on the other was written "hate". They were put away in a closet, under the same condition. Every morning and at night, someone comes to speak to the containers. Only that to the container with the inscription "love", words of love, care and any other nice and soothing confession was made to it. While the container with the inscription "hate", words of hate, rejection, neglect, betrayal and any wrong, awful and unprintable confession were made to it.

In the course of a thirty day period, the containers, being subjected to the same environmental condition, showed a clearly different result. It was noticed that the container with the word "love" written on it was still looking a bit fresh, it maintained it's color and was still a bit appealing to the eyes. While the rice in the container with the inscription "hate" written on it, looked and smelled so bad. Fungi was all over it, and it was all over for that container of rice.

You can also try this at home, so you can see how powerful your words are.

Also, in the ancient Chinese history, whenever a big tree is not needed anymore, it has to be brought down, but for this tree to be brought down, it wouldn't just be cut down, for it might just grow again. So the elders gather around the tree and start cursing it. Yes! They start telling the tree how it's not needed anymore, how it's hated and how everyone wants it to die. Not for long, that tree dies by itself, then they can cut it down.

Think about what you could do with your words of positive confession to your physical beauty that's almost fading away, and anytime you look at the mirror, you feel so depressed. Think about what your constant and continuous confess could do to your weight. If you feel you could loose some weight, why not try confessing the exact weight you want. Think about what your confession could do to your business, to your finances... think!

God, according to his word, created the whole universe with the "word" of His mouth.

Genesis 1:3

And God said, Let there be light: and there was light.

- Kjv

John 1:3

All things were made by him; and without him was not any thing made that was made.

- Kjv

Also, according to God's word, we were created in his "image" and "likeness".

Genesis 1:26

And God said, Let us make man in our image, after our likeness: and let them have dominion over the fish of the sea, and over the fowl of the air, and over the cattle, and over all the earth, and over every creeping thing that creepeth upon the earth.

- Kjv

This dominion handed over to man by God also works in our finances!

All we got to do is act like God! He created us just like himself. If God wants a thing done, He just says it, and boom! It is already there. We are just like him. We also have the creative power of God inside of us. We can create whatever we want. We can speak to our finances to grow, and it obeys. We can speak to that business to respond and yield her increase and it automatically responds.

The Bible says that we are gods, He has made us just like himself, having all the properties and characteristics He possesses.

> *Psalms 82:6*
>
> *I have said, Ye are gods; and all of you are children of the most High.*
>
> *- Kjv*

He is a creative God, that speaks out with his mouth whatever He wants to see. He just says it and it comes to pass. We can also do this. All we have to do is "believe". Whenever you speak it, believe it, and what you believe, you shall see.

For if your mind can see it, and your heart can believe it, and your mouth can speak it out loud, then, it will surely come to pass.

The scriptures made us understand how powerful our words are. How small but mighty our tongue is.

Proverbs 18:21

Death and life are in the power of the tongue...

- Kjv

When you misuse the power of your tongue you live with the negative result.

There was a particular time I needed an amount of money for a certain project. I did not have a plan to raise the money in that space of time, so I resulted to turning to God on the matter. He gave me an instruction on what to do. So I did it. He asked me to keep confessing to myself that I had the money.

I kept doing this, though it sounded crazy and illogical but God works in supernatural ways, so different from the natural line of thought. So there I was up every night and confessing for an hour that I had the money.

You know what happened? On the tenth day, after confessing this for ten

CONSECUTIVE nights, someone I knew told me that a particular person, sent her money and instructed her to give it to me. I had prior, even till date never seen this person, we barely talk, and she was in a very distant country, different continents to be specific.

When I finally got the money and used it for the sole purpose I wanted it for, God spoke to me. He told me "you see son, your confession is very important, it works". This experience I had increased my consciousness and sensitivity to what I say. I know it regulates my life now , so am very conscious to always say the right things.

The only problem is that people lack consistency in this, and most times do not have faith in it, so it does not come to pass.

Have faith. Believe. Be consistent in your positive confession, and it will surely come to pass.

Mind you, just picking one of the principles of wealth creation in itself might not work out. It only works out when you take all in, practicing them consistently. I assure you, there is no one practicing all these laid down principles of wealth creation that is poor.

Go ahead, give it a consistent try, and see the resultant effect. See your finance take a positive dimension!

Don't use your tongue to describe the situation, rather use your tongue to change the situation.

CHAPTER FOUR

How to remain in abundance

A lot of times in life, we notice that there is not much consistency in the financial score board. People do well today, and then fall flat tomorrow, so flat that you barely hear of them anymore. What are they doing wrong?

Well, first let us analyze the reasons for the drop.

1. The foundation was not right.

Just like the Bible says:

> *Psalms 11:3*
>
> *If the foundations be destroyed, what can the righteous do?*
>
> *- Kjv*

If the your business and idea is resting on a faulty foundation, it will one day come crumbling down.

If your multinational corporations is built on a stolen idea, or your business empire was built on capital that has it source from fraudulent activity, it will one day fall just like the walls of Jericho.

You cannot build good on evil. You cannot do good, give to charity, help the needy and all that philanthropic gestures but at the background trafficking drugs or sex slaves, and expect that your empire will last. It will not. Why? Because that foundation is faulty.

Matthew 9:17

Neither do men put new wine into old bottles: else the bottles break, and the wine runneth out, and the bottles perish: but they put new wine into new bottles, and both are preserved.

- Kjv

The Bible also says:

> *Matthew 7:24-27*
>
> *25.   Therefore   whosoever heareth these sayings of mine, and doeth them, I will liken him unto a wise man, which built his house upon a rock:*
>
> *25. And the rain descended, and the floods came, and the winds blew, and beat upon that house; and it fell not: for it was founded upon a rock.*
>
> *26. And every one that heareth these sayings of mine, and doeth them not, shall be*

likened unto a foolish man, which built his house upon the sand:

27. And the rain descended, and the floods came, and the winds blew, and beat upon that house; and it fell: and great was the fall of it.

- Kjv

You have to be likened unto the wise man according to this scripture, that builds his business, idea and career on a rock. That is our safest foundation. The challenges you encounter as you built your career, business and idea are likened unto the rain, flood and the wind in the above scripture. If you have built your empire on the rock, it will surely stand the test of time.

Mind you, the rock being referred to here is Jesus Christ. He is the foundation.

> *Isaiah 51:1*
>
> *Hearken to me, ye that follow after righteousness, ye that seek the LORD: look unto the rock whence ye are hewn...*
>
> *- Kjv*

> *1 Corinthians 10:4*
>
> *And did all drink the same spiritual drink: for they drank of that spiritual Rock that*

This utterly means that if you built your career and empire or even your life as a whole on the rock, the foundation Jesus Christ, you are indeed a wise man and the storms of this life can never bring it down, because it is hinged on something that no element of life can crash.

2. There was no consistency in following the laid down principles.

If there was no consistency, in following the principles we have enumerated and extensively studied above, there is sure to be a dwindle in the financial score board of that individual or business.

Most of the time we start a thing so promising, but later fail to uphold it to the latter, thereby truncating the expected result. Then it looks as though it does not work. It actually does work, if only you can be patient enough to watch it work out.

Remaining and abiding in wealth and riches, means that the principles must be followed, and it must be followed dedicatedly and consistently.

CHAPTER FIVE

Now take delivery

As we conclude this book, it is of great importance to note that wealth creation is very much possible, it is not only possible, but it also possible for every believer. There is no special set of persons wired to be more successful that the other. It all takes the ability to follow the earlier stated principles. However, a primary principle has to be honored.

When we allow God into our lives by

accepting Jesus thereby being born again, we are automatically engrafted into the family of God and entitled to command the same authority God wills to his children. He also takes over the financial issues of our lives, makes all things new, and there will be great ease. Everything becomes easier because He guide and direct us always and we will be able to follow because we hear him.

Remember :

Deuteronomy 8:18

But thou shalt remember the LORD thy God: for it is he that giveth thee power to get wealth, that he may establish his covenant which he sware unto thy fathers, as it is this day.

- Kjv

The only way we can get Him make all things easy in our lives and taking full control of it, is by inviting Him to do so; by becoming born again. When we become born again, our spirit man is then transformed and we become sons of God; joint heirs with Jesus Christ. Then and only then can we enjoy this benefit.

Psalms 82:6

I have said, Ye are gods; and all of you are children of the most

High.

- Kjv

So permit me to ask, are you born again? Have you been adopted into the family of God to enjoy all the divine benefits that comes with it? Have you been redeemed and saved from the horrors of darkness?

If your answer is "no" you can be saved right now, you can be adopted into the family of God. You can live in total freedom from the shackles of poverty and the devil.

According to this scriptural reverence:

Romans 10:9-11

That if thou shalt confess with thy mouth the Lord Jesus, and shalt believe in thine heart that God hath raised him from the dead, thou shalt be saved.

For with the heart man believeth unto righteousness; and with the mouth confession is made unto salvation.

For the scripture saith, Whosoever believeth on him shall not be ashamed.

- Kjv

If Truly you are tired of where you are in life right now and you want God to take over and make all things new and easy for you, causing you to live your life and do all you do from "rest", all you need to do is just to say this prayers with me right now.

There is no distance in the realm of the spirit, God's power will touch you right where you are.

Say this prayer:

Lord Jesus, I thank you for dying for my sins, I believe that you died for me and God raised you from the dead on the third day. I need you now, come into my life and make all things new. Help me as I cannot help myself. All this and more I pray in Jesus name, amen.

If you have sincerely prayed this prayer with faith, you are now born again, Jesus has truly come into your life. Continue in your fellowship with him but make sure you do not keep quite about what He has done for you. Tell your friends, let them know how transformed you are. Give yourself to the study of God's word daily for that is the way you get renewed.

Romans 12:2

...but be ye transformed by the

renewing of your mind, that ye may prove what is that good, and acceptable, and perfect, will of God.

- Kjv

God bless you.